Ronk has always sharply angled her gaze toward the world's unlikely phenomena, revealing and reveling in the heat she detects underneath. In *Silences* she searches for and settles in pauses, stops, breaks, in-between spaces, seeking to "stand for the ambiguity found." What's also found is tension, drama, the story of why and how "the silence after isn't the same as the silence before." She takes inspiration from, and writes about, great artists of interstitial spaces, such as Samuel Beckett, John Cage, Rene Magritte, Mark Rothko, and Vincent van Gogh, and meditations on the practice of ekphrastic art. Photos of refugees attempt to catch people in moments "without a future, without a past," as if it were possible to extend the precious, fleeting present. Ronk gets as close as one can, in these new poems, to dancing on the pinhead of now.

CRAIG MORGAN TEICHER, AUTHOR OF *We Begin in Gladness: How Poets Progress*

One could say the pot is built by spinning a lump of clay away from the emptiness hiding in its center; one could say a painting secretly envisions the light by which it sees what it sees; and one could say, and might need to say, reading Martha Ronk's patient and beautiful *Silences*, that the poem is a portrait of the silence that gives birth to, and carries into the world, words. "Silence isn't an opposite," Ronk writes, but the varieties of silence carry bouquets of contradictions: origins and ends, innermosts and outermosts, the nothing that's not and nothing that is. These poems seek, in humble and honest ways, all that falls back into, or refuses to emerge from, the inexpressible rooted silently inside the givens of our lives—not to break the secret open, but more simply, more wondrously, to admit it's there. Such poems return us to art's fundamental courage: to note where facts and knowledge fray into the unknown from which they were first woven, and to ask those questions that end beyond the end of the poem.

DAN BEACHY-QUICK, AUTHOR OF *Of Silence and Song*

The silence that rules this book touches all the senses, creating a synesthetic web in which the whole body participates. And yet it's also a book of pauses, perceived as suspensions; for just a split second, the reader feels her body slightly left aloft. Throughout, we have no idea what's coming next, not in a sensational way, but instead calmly, and quietly, what comes after is always a perfect fit, and always sends us on to the next unexpected "after"—*afterimage, aftermath, afterthought*, and all that comes *just after* the blackbird's whistling.

COLE SWENSEN, AUTHOR OF *Gravesend*

In *Silences*, Martha Ronk writes us into extremities of detection, the nervy edge of silence, meticulously gathering what falls away in time: missing fantails, reflections of a glass shivering, rainslicked windows, water-polished wood, washed out ventriloquy, blackened nonentity. Virginia Woolf's beautifully observed "Death of A Moth" comes to mind, and Robert Frost's "Directive." The prevailing mode is elegy, but also, a praise-minded litany whose components disband in flight and song, appear and disappear in fog. There are wells of love and sorrow in this book, looked into with patience and undeceived gratitude. I am reminded of Jean-Louis Chrétien's statement in *The Ark of Speech*: "The first hospitality is nothing other than listening"—and of Lorenz Oken's differentiation: "The eye takes a person into the world. The ear brings the world into a human being." Ronk has a rare gift for making vision audible and tactile, and hearing, radiantly refreshing. I love to hear her think. Her many forms of querying silence are gifts to anyone suffering sensory deprivation in the very thick of noise.

SARAH GRIDLEY, AUTHOR OF *Loom*

Recently we have realized that crumpling a sheet of paper results in patterns as complex and as beautiful as origami—this chaos produces patterns in spite of itself. Martha Ronk's *Silences*, the book, contains silences like the varied surfaces of crumpled paper—shimmeringly suggestive of sounds and colors and moods:

> *and what response might there be if silence   should issue forth*
> *into greater and greater density   coalesce into a gesture worthy of being a gesture*
> *or a language   spoken without breath   ("silence of photgraphs")*

For decades now Ronk's has been a project of ethical attention, of paying attention to the shapes and sounds and colors of as many aspects of the world as can be contained in gesture—it is about the most beautiful and responsible project ongoing in poetry today.

BIN RAMKE, AUTHOR OF *Light Wind Light Light*

SILENCES

Martha Ronk

OMNIDAWN PUBLISHING
OAKLAND, CALIFORNIA
2019

Cover art:
Untitled or Before the Curtain: Serenade by Courtney Gregg.
Ink, gesso, and graphite on paper (5" x 7 3/8"). 2018

Cover typeface: Cochin LT Std
Interior typeface: Garamond 3 LT Std

Cover & interior design by Cassandra Smith

Printed in the United States
by Books International, Dulles, Virginia
On 55# Glatfelter B19 Antique
Acid Free Archival Quality Recycled Paper

Library of Congress Cataloging-in-Publication Data

Names: Ronk, Martha Clare, author.
Title: Silences / Martha Ronk.
Description: Oakland, California : Omnidawn Publishing, 2019.
Identifiers: LCCN 2019015242 | ISBN 9781632430755 (paperback : alk. paper)
Subjects: | BISAC: POETRY / General. | POETRY / American / General.
Classification: LCC PS3568.O574 A6 2019 | DDC 811/.54--dc23
LC record available at https://lccn.loc.gov/2019015242

Published by Omnidawn Publishing, Oakland, California
www.omnidawn.com (510) 237-5472 (800) 792-4957
10 9 8 7 6 5 4 3 2 1
ISBN: 978-1-63243-075-5

1. AFTERIMAGE

The shape of silence takes color from a long boat carved from one log,
a color never encountered but close in its eddies to the various blues
of Caribbean waters in a country clearly named but impossible to
paddle days and nights to, slightly curved near the prow and bowsprit
yet from considerable distance a bend straightening towards a line
parallel to the horizon, not unlike the sky in its ability to transform
each half twinning the other as the spectrum hues meet in a circle
the interior of which has been rubbed and sanded so that the surface
mirrors the arch above and the faces that stare into the mica-like silver
their eyes turning to right and left searching for the middle point
are mine and yours as we might have been in our various incarnations
and maneuvers around which the turtle moves slowly carrying
the surface of the ocean on its shell as it swims towards a destination
known solely to each alone but in the communal certitude of silence.

OF TOMORROW THE MIND DOES NOT AS-YET KNOW

To hit "pause" as in reruns having seen it before it keeps on
in the doorway, down the stairs and into the next day
                              the same abrupt halt

imaginings are already fact   I've learned to fear what scurries out
of sight and even what the mind does not yet know

before I remember to adjust the pace   I'm running first
then a step or two
            (and what to call the space between one and the other)

always breaking the most elaborate of plans

film breaks into celluloid   dust or finger smear prevents
knowing who and why and it does something to one's innards as well

                              drops down into

a deadening of sensation or pausing at times staring into space

 no longer desiring one's desires   each event neutralized

as each   steps into a vacancy with no past, no future,
                              only filmic destinations

between the book's main matter and the afterward there's a blank page
a pause before whatever's to come

what will her face look like tomorrow, the day after,

or if pausing in the running so much breathing is going on,
despite detachment,

how much of breathing can one hold   she used to pass out
just to prove a point   a mouth shut tight.

The blackbird whistling or just after
      (from "Thirteen ways of looking at a blackbird"
      Wallace Stevens)

after holds before as in a picture frame,
turned over to the shadow side

 afterimages playing on the brown backing

a memory of birdsound infused with lingering silence,
water charged with brushed out color

a voice left in empty stairwells

the way we say moonless night to yet hold the moon

*

the silence after isn't the same as the silence before,
it's circumscribed by remnants of sound

tactile as fingernails, a contoured attentiveness

leftover notes shaped like water forms
gullies in the sand
             the soundless rasp of crayon on paper

             wax suspended on the roughened surface

nothing infused with something

the silence after is never the before
sliced into as it is by aftermath,

a line through, launched by a trill
vibrating as strings vibrate after plucking

as water pushes against the boy's body as he moves forward
toward a tree shading the stream and the cooler circle of black

(what is it about silence that yet holds unsounded sounds)

in a body that is taking him over, that irritable place
between before and after

components of skin and water

*

silence won
      is made possible when

just after,

standing in front of the Dufy palm the lavender floor tilting

      legs crossing over the legs of garden chairs in imitation

      breath held

it comes as skin sliding into place, the place

of excavating hours,

      and finally all the unseen, unheard stuff of what one is not space opens, not vertiginously

but settled, four-square
                    as lying flat on the ground
            tricks us out of logic

a smudged lilac gives out life as hypothesis
                    as in the painting of his studio, Matisse's
            canvases stacked,

after acting as possibility—scaffolding extended and holding
            the prepared and unpainted in full view

*

it's iconic as the shape of bird
sketched in pencil, order imposed:

hollow circle put in for eye and its linear profile
circle for head, triangle for beak

a simple depiction of the thing itself

if we light a match in the forest it's not to see
but to uncover how much more darkness is around

looming behind trees
behind their skeletal certainty

a leg giving way without warning
the endless fall from one step to what's next

STARTLE

The startle of a bird caught in a photographic blur or its automatic
response to doors and windows only the one open for escape

one's own encrypted and kept for historical files
as technology shifts record endless details in the distant clouds

and in between the failure to hear the others simulates silence broken
as soon as the fledglings are able, falling first and without deliberation

as we halt procedures taken up for good reason and give over
to watching eucalyptus branches, soundless treetops, erasures of phases

its particular cry recorded on an iphone pressed against my ear,
startled by the sound of pleading from whoever I thought I was.

She heard sparrows (Virginia Woolf)

Something making a sound never made before, a series

of slurred whistles in increasing tempo common, uncommon,

invented for the sake of geography, birds of the air, the narrow eye ring

a song from a branch of *artemisia absinthium*

and bathing in indentations, a scattering of wings scattering dust,

the rapidly unforeseen, something not exactly bird-like,

night falling in layers, as the iconic aspect of all things hidden

in paper and feathers, the brushed technique of feathering to absence—

after a time the more they sound like creatures falling

outside the imaginable, rustling, unfolding,

a doubling of moments of having been here before,

a feeling of transparent thickness over-layering,

then the sparrow speaking four or five times prolonged and piercing

in Greek words, from trees in the meadow

beyond a river where the dead walk, *how there is no death*.

A twisted tongue, a sliding horn of meaning, improvising
when it comes to nuance, the arcane closer than the exact,
une pièce d'eau, "a piece of water" once used in English for *pond*
where the gap between the two leads underground,
where the idea of silence has its chance between molten and stony,
between what I thought you said and what you said, what you said
and what you meant, before the alterations of inflected time,
a stuttering repeat, *were you/did you/do you recall*, baffling music
from some else's instrument, stones in the pockets of a wet overcoat.

Now here, now not

After a time the less they seem like what one remembers,

winged creatures falling outside the parameters,

outside the range of vision, a skitter slide under camouflage,

a species destined to decline and vanish,

without which space at our feet remains empty,

no under-table skirmish, where something once was,

nothing, no shadow outlined against a sky,

no flicker and dive, only so many more days—

its forests, marshes, lagoons shrinking to patches,

invasions of oil and plastic, chemical pile up, nerves shaking,

eerie silence where we may never hear paralytic songbirds in a field

and in Delhi no more trees I've never been to.

> *There is no such thing as an empty space or an empty time. There is always something to see, something to hear. In fact, try as we may to make a silence, we cannot.*
>
> John Cage, *Experimental Music.* 1957

Pauses in prose, a jump between paragraph 6 and 7, he to she

or years to they, to graphic signs * or # or indentations to indicate

a breath, an infinitive broken at the line's end as Creeley, "a void of/

pattern," a stutter, he always had a stutter, a held back, it

shuts down speakers, the outloud ones, birds stop to hear another's

response in the in-between that isn't, the jump across metaphysical

metaphors, the question of how this goes with that, holds us silently

near to the pleasure of bafflement, a pleasure of not exactly right-on

unless like a Duchamp *re-contextualized*, how awful a word,

yet moving things about is what we do, erasing, adding, cutting

whole sections of stuff, not to mention "what happened" to

someone, really as they say, the bus going by, someone still in it.

Pauses and synapses: Alice

Inadvertent pauses pile up a random day, first easterly,

westerly, something near at hand, its ungainly shape

no strategy for assessing how voided and looming,

this body insists don't move, steps escalating or shifting

sideways, the far-off foot as foreign as *drink me* or *eat me*,

changing doorways, plot points, a head up a chimney, poor girl,

leaking migraines, flashes of pink and green

brain impulses taking ever longer from brain to limb

what was she looking for, pausing as each turn changed her

into walrus, rabbit, nasty card trick, heads-off queen.

Turning the Pages

Reading pages, then turning the paper aware of the under thumb
or fussing to get 96 not 97, the flap of sound, and the necessary pause
between, being a good reader, knowing that initial views are partial
allowing for no developed thought, but perhaps a catch of the breath
or the pause of trying to turn the pages as slowly, quietly as possible
so as not to wake whoever's sleeping on the other side,
listening to what might "break the silence" and ruin the pause
that reading alone in time, stolen from the dark, from talk
and the day's perpetual latching of one thing to another, allow,
and holding the breath as if it provided loft, hopelessly clutching at it.

SILENCE, A QUERY

what is it&
can it be wedged into words
if spoken
already obliterating
what it is, isn't it
still, how else
&more importantly why
what occurs to us
because of it&brings up
the isolation in
a moment of
call it, lichen imprint
one way of getting at it
its fingers
fringy crust
unnamable tint
&what comes
forward, its twist
&its twistedness in us
all along,
voiceless voices
symbiotic intertwine
silence/noise
whatever allowances
how many or none
what position does it take
cross-legged in darkness
probing the night
is it puzzling
at itself, analog of X
is it some imperfect music
mixed variants
numbers slipping
&in&out

Afterimage

I use afterimage in preference to aporia as a governing term,
however, precisely because such holes are "filled"—not in kind
but in substance—with the vestiges afterimages reliably conjure.
Because these vestiges categorically differ from their visual sources;
they are therefore more difficult to track or tie seamlessly to a narrative,
rather like the movements of narrators they follow idiosyncratic,
nonlinear paths. The afterimage thus undergoes a transformation
of sorts, and yet it retains within it a trace (or several traces)
of its origins. To the extent that it persists independently
of those origins, the afterimage should be understood as a temporal
as well as visual event, one defined—much like the traumatic incidents
upon which the afterimage is often predicated—by an incremental
delay or belatedness. Meanwhile, its lack of concrete materiality
throws it back on the resources of the psyche either to shepherd it
into the realm of sense and knowability or else to abandon it
as one more (potentially insoluble) enigma.

THE SITE OF ORIGIN (AND ANN HAMILTON)

Someone else's memories they must have been
spilling down streets of green paint, hands green, fingers green,
how small her fingernails as if she were an impossible thing
through the dim window looking in at her,
panes palmed and tapped by those caught in tedium—
I can see it all despite the years, but hear nothing,
sound bound to the present, silence to the site of origin,
winding down to events that never happened,
reproduced on a few black and white photos curled at the edges
blank borders of nonexistent futures and the effort to see
how many words, how many years of it, in rooms of paper
as if silence were the protean bed of it all—
in a museum, I walk through a vast room in which reams
fall slowly from the ceiling, fall until our legs mash through
mounds of paper until it piles and keeps piling.

AFTERMATH

Rothko's streak of black paint crosses from left to right
halted by the frame on either side, its linear extension only surmised

and dredged up as a cry comes as a sharp cut in air
                 all that has happened, color coloring sound

                 what is a natural voice
I can't even find it when I'm talking out loud no matter the color
                                 of the sky

afterwords not only pages in books but ones made in air,
on canvas   those iridescent black lines

a distant voice calling used to be a bedroom each of us slept in
out there out the window of what comes next,
                 birds, crying crows

if nothing in words can be visual, what's sound on a page
and yet below the black is gray or orange, a kind of silent enigma

                 so many colors

like sounds merging, one's own and a washed-out ventriloquy
                 liquid moving

as balance wavers, a glass of water on an outstretched hand

                 as turning silent in the midst of speaking as hearing
voices slipped in, no longer able to speak   sitting in the dark listening

                 to the highly purpled air, streaks of maroon.

ELEGY

No single image, only the landscape of afternoon,
a time not merely of time but lifted from a color of space

if space were shaded with colors within our range of vision,
it rises in paper folds, claims grief from her hardbound copy

of Greek gods, sliding into the inescapable as a jut of land
slides into the surrounding sea, arriving at headstones

with local names of the dead—as she draws closer in rooms
disappearing first from the oldest in memory

as erosion takes the hillside where we went to see a ruin
by the sea and stumbled into all we thought to avoid

by means of a landscape nothing of our own
the afternoon climbing out of itself,

names incised in concrete, her far-flung hair,
a sort-of voice and habits reminiscent of the human race.

No such thing as empty space or an empty time, there's always

something, no way to create silence as Cage tells it,

in an anechoic chamber at Harvard, hearing two sounds,

one high and one low, the high one being, the engineer said,

his nervous system, the low one, the circulation of the blood.

"Until I die, there will be sounds" until I die, those hummings stalkings

unfoldings one on top of another, a cerulean collagepiece

lost in the layers of drawer paper pasted over the stunned silence

of arms and legs, rendered still, more than still,

set backwards into a category of the not-having come-into-being,

bloodless forms of pure flesh, circles of naked skin,

a hand on a shoulder, hands pointing to the inscription,

a hand loosely draped over marble, no sound,

not a whisper from the missing fantails blown in from somewhere.

MAGRITTE: *THE KISS*

To restore silence is the role of objects

Samuel Beckett

Nothing looks the same or walks the same these latter days,
this face looking only to where it's going, the coffee high,
the arching neck, the palm tree cracking the concrete once called to me,
now clouds cover the surface of what's moving slowly,
missing milkweed fluttering its orange wings seems to have
nowhere to go, to avoid nearing what isn't there:
a face behind twisted cloth facing a lover, those wrapped-up
head-like things, muffled in their winding sheets
while behind them in the upper right corner a detail of molding.
Ordinary, luminous, wry.

MAGRITTE: *THE EMPIRE OF LIGHT*

Tree shadows finger the fading sky with probes into the blue clouds
all cut from the same "how to" for children, the gaiety of sky belied

by heaviness below, darkness surrounding house lights, a single
street lamp, walking home late winter afternoon the sound of leaves

her only reassurance against never arriving, never being sure,
new directions dissolving into windy sounds, unformulated trees

in the late day in the sound of tires, static on the distant radio,
bushes on either side of the road cramming together their greens—

exactitude a means to contain the overpowering:
rectangular houses with rectangular windows and yellowish light

on either side of the afternoon reassuring the girl that it is the world,
was the one of yesterday, might be the one tomorrow.

A GIRL RUNNING (AND *MYSTERY AND MELANCHOLY OF A STREET* DE CHIRICO)

Arches puncture the white arcade, blackened despite light that whitens

as it descends, blasts into incised shadow—flattened cutouts emerge,

buildings slip from their concrete and lower below the threshold,

we've crossed the divide between one ochre and another, a trauma

no child can comprehend, as side-stepping the openings of arches

and carriage wheels, the girl's running in the windowdressing

of sunlight, while the soldier stands ominously silent

at the end of the diagonal, raising the inevitable shadow lance.

Winter (The Vicarage Garden Under Snow) **Van Gogh**

The painting's quiet, lowers below all sound
the threshold we must have crossed over, that river dividing
the tracks from the bridges, from the unrepresented town
as we stand there about 4pm in front of the white snow
dirt coming up from under the once white cover and a man shoveling
his angled body—behind him the river and branches lightly dusted,
more twiggy things than could be counted unless standing as still
and long as the man, the branches trying for movement
in their jagged horizontals, but still, unmoving
and the effort to be where one is not amplifies silence
the effort to wipe out the noises of shoes, murmurs, a coat
coming off, to stand alone with the scene in which the shovel
can't lift the wet snow, the river can't run,
and the vicarage garden lies below the frozen ground.

OTHERS (AND VAN GOGH'S *BEDROOM*)

The one sitting there, the one who's the one about whom some slivers
of what one can ever know might be known—

    yet unreadable on a backdrop up for grabs, even the color

as when the label calls the walls "violet" now chemically altered
to blue in the painting of a bedroom,

as I look up and see a woman, herself fading
                    (a headache of green and pink
into voice
    how effort can't find them or move them closer

no wonder silence crawls up folding chairs,
folds us in deep crevices, some intimate, some farflung languages
    of the underskin, the specific finger taps

and how *rosy fingered dawn*, could break someone's heart,
    still I'll never understand suicide no matter how I try,

deep silence behind one's own straining to grasp who he was,
or might have been,
    his conjugation of verbs and the stale smell of brick,

as opaque as one's own efforts to imagine being out of air
    but for the temporary cessation in which time must extend

into claustrophobia, where proximity falters and tilts the objects

in the room: cane chair, bottles of who-knows-what, red-green floor,
reflections of
    a glass slivering.

RUINS (AND YEATS)

A stone ruin, a stone opening barred to keep some in, some out,

open to cries of ravens, rain, crowds, the frail with their tipped canes

over uneven ground, stepping into vacancy, wrists in motion,

then a lapse, wind off the bayside, a tangled waste of landscape,

an awkward grope for balance, the color of slate

or the nondescript color of sand between wet and dry,

as the sky turns murky, a smear in the garments of manuscripts

silent in vitrines or the shapes of monks walking a mountain

to a hut beyond—they have yet to discover whatever formulation

of truth they were in the midst of as they trudged upwards –

various formations of clouds over the jagged landscape—lazurite blue.

Ruins in Ireland

What are they, silent in their uninterrupted stone, a monument

to Benedictine isn't enough despite labels for refectory, fireplace, nave,

where we're standing in a marked-off field holds its own beyond us

with the stone figure seated up in a corner, eroded features,

as ashes left alive after flame

when monks walked the round of grass, built a columbarium,

did what they did, the shape's always the shape it is,

shattered bits lying about, ruined windows of sky,

pigeons still around, flapping.

A PAINTING OF A MAN READING SILENTLY

What makes the move from sound to silence on the pages
open before him, eyes moving left to right, having to learn to do it

    without sound

used as they were to sermons, speeches, the painter painting the move
into silence, a finger laid across his mouth,

    (the ocean never silent, only inattention
                allowing for shutting it off)

I no longer read the books I used to read every year, now closed
next to others on the bookcase shelf built in a commotion they left

    leaving silence and the question of relation

hanging as an apparition   (as in ultramarine, "beyond the sea")

these unfamiliar marks on a page now lacking any sound,

a swell of words, rising and falling as he goes it alone.

Over time (after T. J. Clark on Poussin's "Landscape with a Calm")

To return to the changing light in the silent room,

trying to see a painting differently, slowly each time,

revising, turning his eyes to another figure, another color,

the way a small V arrows into the space between glance

and sight, shapeshifts to maneuver the invisible narrows,

a painting's self-sufficient containment resistant to probe,

turned away from exposure and the limits of time.

Example #1, passing by, example #2 returning January-June

looking again until an opening opens,

an occurrence such as blue, locked eyes, a detail of horse and rider

off to the side, the way it startles and hadn't been there before,

goes in a direction out of the painting as if insignificant,

almost missing given the speed of the horse, and a tiny conundrum—

finally seen, an arm reflected in the lake, nude, watered over

> *Language is always too specific and discriminating, it seems, when it tries to mimic the first idiotic appropriation of the visual.*
> T. J. Clark

AN OPERATION OF EARTH AND MOON

Why do we do what we do, what we don't,

yanking at the ineffable and off-register,

as it keeps its distance moving off as slow wind,

coming in steadily errant, so much weather,

whenever I move I keep standing where I stand,

caught in sickly green, heels dug

when I ought to be coming in a front door,

something unnamable takes over

following in the footsteps of others gone before

a stormsurge of couldn't help it

as across the way in the oily motorwater

of Five Mile River I'm caught in an operation

of earth and moon, unable to resist the wet dark

moving steadily out into the wet dark.

SILENT MOTIVES

Mud flats, fog, beaten tree limbs out the window
a lecture tonight on "rising seas" in Samoa's women's club
needing paint she tells me as she brings the mail by
lowlands at risk, *uprooted* a way of seeing, walking off the narrow,
slipping into geography's weedrange, wheat-colored grasses
getting by or backed into as never saying anything
about what pits or zones open later in the day or next
as we drive away from the coast and up towards the meteor shower
never getting to it behind the fog bank, how I like the idea I read
of the *wind/body problem* but for me it's the slant of pushing against
leaning into or turning to the other side as when it's all I wanted once
was the other side of the wall it was everything I didn't know—
she says Manila won't be flooded in twenty years as the seawaters
continue to rise, memory to fade, but I keep coming back to
the tree placed just there without motive, without window in mind.

Ekphrasis

Silence contains everything in itself. It is not waiting for anything, it is always wholly present in itself and it completely fills out the space in which it appears.

Max Picard

A *speaking picture*, impossible silence, out of which oceans, debris,
that undulating wing in the breastbone, in headswamp, low down
as water level, swampy tides, a still life spilling jagged architectures
of white cloth over a table, the torqued effort of blue, ochre,
the serif towards which she is heading, a leg lifted towards the gallery
shifting the weight of a body disappearing into crayon
and back again, staring into a figure posed and self-contained,
yet what's this back and forth between us and what to make of
someone who paints the face of the man who is painting, staring into
his own eyes, or of the pull of a silent rectangle, an unpainted bit
gripping tight, inexhaustible as yearning, unhooked from standing here.

silence measured in ....

                              defined by the
                    surrounding....
sorely needed for purposes of...

                    and often ignored in ....

more prevalent in.....   fearful when, hateful to,

unencumbered thereby

2. ARCATA CALIFORNIA: SILENCE AND FOG

Sometimes it's good to fall into emptiness. Be it another person, or oneself, or a junkyard...Blessed are the hours of emptiness. My life vacillates between the two, the emptiness and... and... whatever is the opposite of it.

Jonas Mekas

A slough at the trail's end, once another world and, now
quiet, no logs rail lines cattle
only watermarsh, not even waterfowl
mere vacancy and my own
imposed.

For years I've thought, *words beget words*, silence forgets them, not
erases, but mirrors them, like quarter note written on fogged windows, an
eighth, sixteenth, until they move around one another, skimming the top
of water, pushing duckweed slightly aside. A metallic sheen is the surface
of the water at the marsh as light begins to fade. Jigsawed out of farm lands
and grazing land to restore lagoons and wetlands, the marsh is part of a
wastewater project, the ooze of water and ponds spreading out to support fish
and oysters harvested from lagoons, deeper in some spots, shallower in others.
Filled with Hardstem bulrush and Sago pondweed seeds it draws birds to the
small islands: herons, cranes, grebes sinking halfway below the surface as if
going under, never going under, cormorants, Cooper's Hawks, this quiet place
begetting itself and, ironically, words.

Books speak in the middle of the night connecting the fictional and
what's called the non-fictional worlds, the living and the dead, both of whom
move closer in the dark. Even watching someone climb the stairs is a first act
leading somewhere as the plot always does, connecting scenes up, positing
coherence, once called Fate. I wish I could escape the narrowness of life, speak
another language or select experiences I never had, setting the day going in
unexpected ways, singing a baritone, waking in a foreign land. So, I take up
silence and a book with paper pages on my knees and acknowledge there is
no way to unthink oneself from what I am and what I am is often what's been
read, all those pages now inside and of approximately the same size if size
were a steady concept as it isn't, but ranging about, expanding, contracting.
Years pass and I have to read the same book again, both of us now different. I
am asked why I have to read before sleeping, but it's so obvious I could never
explain.

Ever-present fog deletes houses, lays down a backdrop for cypress, myrtle, Queen Anne's lace; any upstanding twig darkens, an outline of black branches so precise it seems to define the morning. A cell phone passes by loping with the boy's gait, "rap" in, then out again to soundlessness, a quiet backed by distant logging trucks, fewer each year. Something about fog enervates. One feels limp and unstructured and I find myself thinking about motivation, the boy's, my own—what does it in, what weight in the shoulders, or what makes for pressing urgency—the urgency I've felt, an acid and indigestible insistence, remembering the dirty face of the Queen Anne's lace taking the field on that other coast with whatever wind years ago. Taken over by fog I can't see what's in front of me but I think of following the white line in the road without ever doing anything I've always done again. I tell myself I don't want to use analogy, yet it recurs, furrows in the water sweeping the shore matching their finny lines in patterns as light sweeps over them, light fading with the earth's turning, walking the vacant beach for miles.

What portent exists in the *cul de sac* we find ourselves in as it grows dark—backwater junkyards of debris, crumpled car doors, the bass moan of hounds and toothless mouths, drugged silence and trash and whose perspective is this anyhow, yet wasn't it what was there, no lights in the windows, the road disappearing in the fogged dark following wires and telephone poles, the stony human silence—close by murky waters under which once there were fish, surveillance hovering the air, wired, planted, scoped and telescoped. Such silence unsettles and I'm filled with guilt, fear, exiled from a gait I thought my own. I am an intruder here, an unwelcome voyeur and no way to help it, no way to blend in.

Down the road towards Eureka the shack by the railroad tracks was burned out from under the guy who sat there and stared out at the Bay day after day and I wonder was it the same guy who planted the rosebush by the encampment, and was he the same as the kid whose family parked its cars in a circle, "covered wagons" protecting them from what might come out of the night and yet what is really in a night when, paranoid, we can't keep from adding to it.

So many hours staring at the sea, its ins and outs—fishermen dying while crossing the bar before the jetty was built. It seems years ago when I was staring at the sea with my father. What was I doing then and how much more could I have done including the various revisions of fact and mind, both eating up time on earth. Staring like this makes it all seem, as we say, of no matter. Yesterday we watched monks in a Buddhist documentary, all of them acting as one, picking tea, praying, planting pumpkins, body and soul weary, as they tuck robes under their feet, harvest tea, their embrace of *emptiness* a factor of motivation as if there were time enough to do it all again as we ate spinach from a weedy patch and I thought how long life isn't long enough, and another voice asks, for what?

The fog over unpainted houses, wilting hollyhocks, black and blacker cypress blurring to sightlessness such that my breath halts more with each step down the unlighted road to the Bay, its muddy flats emitting overwhelming smells of seaweed dank—how old must I be before *I'll never know* becomes as familiar as shapelessness—yet while I'm walking in the dark, the shapely arc of an angel's rainbow drapery shows up as a mental image out of Jacobo Bassano, "The Flight into Egypt," its perfection put there unbelievably by paint, the marvel of a visual retort, no words.

You know if the music you don't want to hear, a favorite such as Lorraine Lieberson singing Bach, you know you're caught in an ache both psychological and physical, ancient as today's winds, rain, indeterminate as unspoken undercurrents, the way pain underlies a body's stillness, interrupting it in levels doctors think can be numbered so you say something to her for the chart, but a swath of colors might be more telling—extended gray in various shades as the weather blocking the moon's move over the sun this morning as we stood around looking up at the eclipse, damp underfoot, most others plugged in as if we'd already left the visual age behind in Fellini's filmed dance on the beach, antiquated as his *Circus of Sadness*, soon a phrase merely metaphoric. Beyond so much else weather stymies. What have we to utter or take in given the relentless size of it over all available surfaces.

Silence isn't an opposite. It's a thing in itself on which blackbirds, whining truck wheels, and undefined voices scrawl shapes like the profiles coming up behind eyelids, an unfamiliar/familiar succession of faces from oblique angles, one into another but never quite gone. They're always in waiting as I close my eyes and must attend to irregular oscillations of outline and inlets. Sometimes I have a sense of recognition, but then the faces turn into strangers or reproductions like the one that's part duck, part old woman. This seems a kind of seeing from some parallel, often emblematic universe and I wonder what for and for how long.

In the novel, the character Jane Eyre uses physiognomy to analyze aspects of character, reading those around her as she had once read the illustrated book of birds. Early on she sees into Rochester by seeing his face: "He had a dark face, with stern features and a heavy brow; his eyes and gathered eyebrows looked ireful and thwarted just now." I'm reminded of potent experiences I had during my years in school of voices heard as what I can only describe, ironically, as deep silence, transfixing, mesmerizing. I would find myself as if felled into some of them, as the lecturer spoke of China, Yeats, *The Winter's Tale*. An unbeliever, I felt as rapt as I imagined believers must be. Attuned somehow to pitch or tone, I was encompassed, gone into them, suddenly missing, written on. It was all in the voice; a kind of fever and potency enveloped me...then time swallows these experiences, leaves them back there somewhere as if they never were.

The silence in Arcata becomes attention to the slippage of time, half-remembered memories of being lost somewhere, of lichens, snake grass, and sand, light turning down a notch, noticing my hands as water drains through them, noticing breathing, sweeping the floor, staring at the fog and sea, bits of wood water-polished, a dish I'd made in the ceramics studio. In an outlandish dream "she" gave me a box of what I remember this morning as a *glory* or that was its name in the dream, a *glory* left over from saints weeping their songs. My sister asks where shall we live later on, how much later on, and what if we aren't able to decide, time passing more quickly as the years pass, bodily memories in limbs we have no choice but to abandon. I think of the silence here as a deep well of "unbelief," both out there and inside, the sea's susurration so rhythmic it wipes itself out and oneself.

It is from zero, in zero, that the true movement of being begins.
Malevich

3. Disquiet

An alternate universe

It shadows you in an alternate universe of everything the same,
exactly the same corridors into which darkness echoes
its own expansion, the fretful beforehand as a dull prod—
see there severance, see there binding, see an overabundance of,
yet exactly as the most ordinary of the ordinary, daily duplicities—
how you awoke and found that ruin was the coin of the realm,
arcane vocabulary and a tone of stridency close to the inconsolable,
rampaging at the ends of its fragility: slabs forced into hillsides
to keep them from sliding as sickly algae spreads over the watercolors
in ponds as ruin grows out of it, the biologically determined
now determining its own, extinction our only trope.

VERTIGO

A return of vertigo tangled in wallpaper patterns,

antlers in the corners of carpets, woven tree shapes in wool,

the necessary reminder to myself, *these are stairs*,

our figures still locked in the friction of each other's ways,

old rooms now whitewashed over, the window tree drooping

its bafflements of years, changes as abrupt as fingerbones cramped

with what they've become, rents too dizzyingly high

according to the economist half of wages, according to another

the problems of trade deficits, all more than mere sounds,

as shoulders dragging, unpaid hours extending, ending in

one foot after another, louder the child, heavier up the stair.

SILENCE (AFTER AUDEN)

Even gibberish dispels despair.

The recitation of facts is one man's way

beautifully spent like slippery coins.

The plot twists and untwisting

takes hours between the two of us.

In the silence the ogre reaches

into the cavity and pulls the entrails out.

In the silence you fall into

the exasperation of the bland

a smiling villain, undeterred.

AGUES AND FUGUES

Under the weather would put one
just about left of the cirrus and right of
the objective correlative,
would locate the ague
in earlier centuries, beneath
the armpit, soaking in a hot tub
as the cloud cover lifts and finds
its place and dizzily high
before beginning again, its fugue.

PROPERTY

Who belongs to whom and where as the bird's noise

to some shrub near the ribs, under the third branch

from the ground, hooked to wings it seems to have flown,

belonging now to the pure form of light in which nothing

makes any sort of sound just skirmish in the dirt,

half-hearted footnotes recalling lists of names on the page of a book

belonging once to others lost in cities belonging nowhere

documenting everywhere as rapidly as mania can manage

where belonging might mean billions offshore, percolated, pretended,

the profitable poison of carbon dioxide, ozone, and methane,

as high-flown sounds fade and slip out and around us:

to whom do they belong these birds sounding their directional language

unknown, unlabeled, belonging to the as-yet unpropertied air.

To whom the air, the birds of the air, flocks skimming

the shoreline, the noises just past what I can hear

the sounds of trains, beyond and belated as a century

belonging to who rules, was ruled, was laying the rails,

shooting the worker, mining for gold, silver

and whose land was taken, whose ways caught on,

who owned those run-ragged and run out of town,

an entire ghetto wiped out after a bar brawl

visible now in the local museum: repros of vintage postcards,

and dead things with glass eyes stuffed and preserved,

muted sounds strangled as history and cries in other tongues,

foreign as the beating of wings.

Unintelligible

Birds haul loud and louder trees

into the middle of the street

where morning here means

closing in, dismissal of all afterthought

in the clatter of branches,

the up and down of a frantic leaf,

out there pollution off freeways

breathes into a child still digging a hole

to China with a spoon

dusty sparrow, dusty crust wrestle together

under tables on sidewalks

unintelligible birdsong.

ELEGY: HER VOICE

Is it louder or quieter, music I thought I'd heard only blood

beating in my ears, only the sound of her voice slipped in

and why we're drawn to rainslicked windows smudging trees

as they speed past and drift us into a ramped up recall

of shoulders and arms and you almost hear the color of sand

where each foot print slides from friction into sound

and out again as shutting the eyes to imprints of flattened seas,

crescendos at a distance, the rising and falling of tides

incremental and invisible as the forces turning us

from flood to drought, as increasing silence

opens a space for her voice easing vocables on the air.

After (and Agnes Martin)

What was I doing on the floor, rag in hand and how many times

the stain of underglaze, rust on the underside of a porcelain sink,

and it happens time after time as the pale color of sun

rises in her canvases just under the surface,

but coming as if there were an *after* in the dawn,

we try to gather just that on paper, spread it on bodies still asleep

knowing what even the splay of an arm will bring,

after is what we have to live with and it moves itself back and forth

in mechanized brainwaves unable to stop what was, what will be

when silence ravishes the sidewalk, takes on the street,

a back and forth ancient body pulling time, pushing it into the future,

a box with wheels filled with bits of bark and leaves

where *after* ghosts itself on the present—take it, amplify it,

see it coming. We all dream the dream of falling.

Naming the blank

Familiar as her own voice working to name the parts
a constriction between rib and rib, the mash-up of irregular verbs
and a fading cerulean blue, a grid, a mark, we guess it's a Manet,
a Martin, a Twombly *painted for his time in a cooperative venture of sorts,*
out of what stuff does it come, go, wordless in corridors
and what's that peculiar light, that suffused horizon
and who's gesturing as she does one shoulder dropped behind
trying to name the unrecognizable creature now speaking,
silent in the fluidity of moving fingers, heads turning around,
she raises her arms, pretends to fly, and why can't I name her
say it over and over as the child humming: rooster, llama, lamb.

3X5 PHOTO OF A HOTEL ROOM

The flat surface into and out of an out-of-body crossing into the past,
a rectangular barrier passed through, permeable, enough to slip into
a supposition of a shape on the edge of a bed, folded over as someone
with a camera records it, flattened by all that happened, barely enough
room for two bodies and a camera circling, space collapsing into a 3x5
piece of paper and a lens-flare of window light, silence in which
no words were spoken, unreliably documented—
flashes heavy as hands.

BREATHLESS

Nefés, a Turkish word for breath

Pina Bausch

A dancer dragging her arms across the stage, slapping feet through a
watery pool
        panting from a bent body,

slamming a body not one's own yet seemingly one's own against a wall,
        eyes cast into blankness, walled-off heaves of breath,

you hear it, feel it stretch the sides of the chest, strain the lungs

again she slams herself into the wall and falls to the floor
        a heaped-up pile of skin and satin slip—

you're not doing anything except not breathing,
        as unnatural a pose as the way she lifts an awkward heel
                lowers it slowly down in limbs not your own,

everything moving faster than thought, that space inside the skull
that isn't a space,
but placed you once beyond legs, arms, walls
            wherever anyone was—

not thinking of it, just being it, as she repeats each gesture
        that arm overhead, elbow out, down against the cheek,

           lift of knee, gracelessly supple, repeated—

a space conceived as if by some mythic creature,
        whose quicksilver calls forth breath, song, ode,

           pushing to the wall the limits of a body

strained to its utmost, gathered as if clouds could be brought to heel

slamming against walls, floors, her own breath open-mouthed
        air dissolving into air out there up there not your own.

VANISHING

                                cloaks wound around shoulders

dragging, unwrapping,   all the purposeless of the necessary—

would it were cold, would it were snow   archaics proliferate

as if language might recreate
                                        a leap in the air

            breathing when she could be swept away out of reach

                            now vanished in more ways than
one body can take it

the stairs longer, the cartons more than cardboard,
                            sounds added/ deleted,

                marking time, interrupting herself,

finds the doorjamb elbow   hears a body

crack of bone   breathless child in the furze of weed

                                airborne,

limp as   tendrils, piled on legs, arms, bones

ON THE PHONE SHE SAYS

Furrows, she says, are forming her brow, lines of insistence

spoken, unspoken, speeding across her skin

as the unruly seeps through all the bulwarks of music, memory,

the lines of inattentive reading, inattentive finches in the rosemary,

murderous crows—embodied in response to scattershot noise

a ricochet through nighttimes and responses to who isn't there

the noise grinding through airwaves she says her mouth

won't work right, silence retreated behind brainwaves,

silence lost to aliens incorporated, the enemy is us,

the tweeted fingers, the ache of tooth and nail, the cyber-

incursions newly detected, and the insensate now sensate.

PHOTOGRAPHS OF REFUGEES
'Shefna el mot bi oyouna,' 'We saw death with our own eyes,'

A photo spread across the center divide imitates enormity,

black and white sea ridges, erupting surfaces in constant motion

ongoing and endless to the edge of the page where chalky sky

takes over, in the far distance a rubber raft crammed low in the water,

two men drag themselves after days at sea,

struggling to pull from the shallows, weighted by winter coats,

space blankets reflecting light folded over the shoulders

of a woman shading her eyes, intent on what can't be seen,

the photographer writes he's only a witness to the surge,

Idomeni 2015—. . . what *is* witnessing, as if in and out

in and out of the sea, in a distant room unable to pull away.

SILENT PHOTOGRAPHS

groups huddled, murmurings worn

to a pseudo-silence, the wrappings of scarves

holding shoulders in more-than-tight,

silence despite what must be the background,

what we know of explosions, how little we know

where no bridges, no way to be pulled into no breathing

remember when she said, he has no empathy,

must be on the spectrum, she said,

multitudes stilled in rubble, unbreathing

News photos

Filling airways with afterward, what then, what next,

pouring out what victims, responders, blocked by airpower

landmines, winds pummeling insubstantial everything

and beforehand the sloughed-off resignation of what might have been

given the weight of forethought, heading off neglect, inertia,

the sleepy ease of *in the long run*, what we've gotten ourselves into,

corruption in the collapsed-in school, no going back to fix it,

just the surge of a wallow we're used to,

boxes of old clothes, street marches for a few days,

stills on a table.

PHOTO OF MEDITERRANEAN REFUGEES

an image comes back and haunts us, two women bent into strong wind,
side by side in black coats, their backs to the camera,
the sea to the right, her cane to the left, barren land abutting the sea
no faces, no voices, turned away from those in the foreground,
looking out, faces grey, mouths frozen and downturned,
in the foreground a boy pulls the sleeves of his sweater
over his hands or puts them in his pocket or the hand-me-down
covers them, anticipation stalled in the silence of *Sep-Dec 2015*,
without a future, without a past, one of the two women
caught with a foot in the air, just walking away,
although what looks implacable, one foot after another, can't be—

GREEK PHRENËTIKÓS, FRANTIC

Silence isn't stillness, agitation has me in its grip
remember reading the Greeks were like us
restless   underneath   and again underneath
water wearing away   crevices   the itch
of canyons   skin I didn't outgrow as
the doctor said   burns hot and stings
allergic to what I bring to it   allergic to
what I'm thinking   how much older
the underpass is   filled to overflowing
blue tented absence   corners with the leftover
plastic and cardboard   happens so fast   it isn't
even my heart that's   broken,
time stealing   and leaking the blue cold
what it would have been to be   Greek
no cortisone   a body   historians
thought women leaky   restless   for what
out of one's own   skin   a future they never
knew who'd have thought   a daily underpass
so many leftovers   left near the parking
pizza   fries   what skin were we wrapped in.

CREATURELY

how to think   or think I've been thinking   and how to

locate where one is   here in this   density

a word husk   roots larger than houses splayed open

light   a mere shaft   not what we saw wherever it was

telephone wires in the redwoods,   the almost new

                a crisscrossing age creases the bark

wheeling over, silent   we know insistence   slight neckbones

looking up

                dangling silence   a faint hum

rocking feet   dusty motes rearranging in the single shaft

what's myself solely underfoot   head wheeling upward

the silent unseen uppermost branches out of which another looms

             how to think we think here,

unlocatable in any arrangement of words

nothing but underfooted many-footed   neck-boned

     leafless and thought-weary creatures

     light-colored dusting upthere

LOST

lost in what I was working on   standing stock still
some finch might fly off   gravel-lifted where I couldn't see
color deepening as in sky   wobbling through its several meanings

in such drought, the trees won't color   as autumn comes on
too dry it says   and down the street she says they just go
from green to brown   methane concentrations upping the heat

re-staining the horizon   fire and smoke along the long state
herds of grazing animals into feed lots   used to count them
from the backseat   up to 20 sometimes on Ohio farmland

demented he repeats the rounds of how   he'll plant a garden this year,
get a hound, fix those broken windows   write about the mirror
his love gave him   one of those "sick" mirrors scarred black

and aluminum-bright   vegetables this year, peas coming early
I trying not to say I'd heard it all before, doubted it all, wished for it all
to be so, that I could attend as he   all of it new, all of the time

Obscurity without color, the night of Brassai means diffusion,
trees invading washes of light, smears of pale liquid
laid across crippled trunks, shadowing a brick wall,
throwing branches into pools, catching light, blocking light,
silhouetted limbs extended, jointed and blackly akimbo,
catching me across the face in rapt fullness, nothing else
lives up to it, of course I'm dying, of course I've hated who I am
and I know the limits of the medium devoted to seeing,
the sins of seeing visited upon me both morning and night,
oh window, oh caught-in-the-fog trees, blackness wrapped
in up-to-the-moment vestments, posed as are the prostitutes
mannered in all their café forms, faces, legs, corsets
all a smash-up of obscurity through breaks in the fog.

INTERPRETATION

means what obscurity always means
could stand for the ambiguity found
where no one could find you,
geographically hidden
and one's amorphousness blessedly
the one wrestling the angel

then two men arranged details in orange
geraniums, cosmos, the blue-with-light
lunar moth flattened as if planted there
from their door to mine nightly
and under the wooden plank of a bed
the meaning of how I'd found myself

sitting it out in the impenetrable air
through letter-sized panes of glass
blackness welled up each time night was
the gender of solitude, pages of *memento mori*,
the Rorschach press of found metal

fitting under the mattress, slapping my face
hard, adolescent configurations vividly tactile,
one of them deconstructed the dream as if he knew
since night had been his all along
as he unfolded sheets from the lawn

it's thicker somehow the silence of photographs, amplified,
turned up, strands blowing piecemeal into layered extensions
strained efforts at dialogue weighted by intention

like paintings but missing the documentary weight of Brassai's photos
"little boxes of night," hints of information charged and conveyed
to someone out there expecting to reply

I hold still as possible staring at black and white more tropic than color
in front of extended pinpoints of multiform gray, grayish
backing into anonymity, blackened nonentity

and what response might there be if silence should issue forth
into greater and greater density, coalesce into a gesture worthy of being
a gesture or a language spoken without breath

absent polyphony out of Tallis or Palestrina heard despite silence
despite trying although it might be trying that edges into thickening,
a portmanteau word, *slithy* perhaps, an overcoat grown heavy in the rain

SILENCE, EDGES OF

Where's the nervy edge of silence, where the slippery *here*,
an idea I had of failure's plentitude and a room I had to be alone in
and there was no such thing

I thought to be standing against a tree, breathing as it does *in and out*
or trying out place names, ease myself in, slowing to press hard
against the bark

we're living in a disappearing world he said in his email from last year,
I was looking for his address to say I wouldn't be coming this year

the arbor and clematis gone, rhododendron against window panes,
the oak tree propped with metal poles, heavy, scarred by age,

waterlogged branches slip into a riverbed, a swirl around a stone,
a typed letter edging in, *sirwl*—a new word for silence, plausible as any

why did I leave the books in the cabin in Vermont, bound,
of course, in the winters to rot

coming to it out of language, the fonts of matter, impressions
into soft paper, what conventions would do it, what shapes, forms,
lines, absences, words could ever capture it

what conventions could be taken up and jagged lines don't cut it

doesn't silence seem to you a murky black, a soft matterless material

or what of the suggestive silence of round-about or breakage
or negatives, no noise, no wind, either a word appears or it doesn't
(Cage argues there's no "doesn't," ever) and what of Celan's
tortured phrases—

is silence concomitant with them, or what about combinatory or
jammed up and what does it mean, "appear"

and if shared ideas about meanings are disappearing and I don't
understand or you don't is that silence and I'll never write anything
so fervent or obscene as to silence the room

or what of silencing oneself by the idea of disappearing into another,
i.e. she couldn't speak for feeling the other woman's hair, her eyes,
her lilting voice

or we might propose not an absence but a something in and of itself
and could it be taught, letting static of mind go, practicing zazen
every day at 5:30 she says, so she left it all behind and moved in

the painting is closed to me, the acrylic, the chalk and pencil
and that patch over there no matter how long I take to sit and stare
as T. J. Clark does, he says.

Cezanne cut a slice out of the wall to take the largest canvas into
natural light: did he say so, what if it's never said to someone else,
and if the book is closed is there no one?

My thinking about silence has been influenced by having summers in the silence of Arcata, California, by silence in museums, by reading about the loss and silence of birds, by the work all the artists named here, especially Wallace Stevens whose poem, "Thirteen Ways of Looking at a Blackbird," initiated this project, by discussions with friends and the reading of other poets to whom I am most grateful. Other reading included Susan Sontag, "The Aesthetics of Silence": "Instead of raw or achieved silence, one finds various moves in the direction of an ever-receding horizon of silence—moves which, by definition, can't ever be fully consummated." She also writes of our need for silence in "unwholesome" times. Influenced by this essay I wrote a short piece on "silence" "Why Poetry Now" for *The Brooklyn Rail*, ed. Ann Lauterbach, October, 2008.

Jean Baudrillard, "Photography or the writing of light," trans. Francoise Debrix
Dan Beachy-Quick, "Lyric Consciousness," *Poetry Northwest*, 1.7. 2018
Samuel Beckett, *The Unnamable*
Rachel Carson, *The Silent Spring*
T. J. Clark, *The Sight of Death*
Giles Duley, *I can only tell you what my eyes see, Photography from the Refugee Crisis*
James Fennimore Cooper, *The Pioneers*
Peter Wohlleben, *The Hidden Life of Trees*
Dale Wright, *What is Buddhist Enlightenment*

Chris P. Miller University of Chicago on silence, online
online accounts of the loss of sparrows in India
Bridget Stuchbury, *Silence of Songbirds*

http://passengerpigeon.org/exhibits.html and the catalog for the Dia exhibit on the Passenger Pigeon

Enormous thanks to my editor and publisher, Rusty Morrison, and to the entire Omnidawn staff.

Thanks to those who read earlier versions of these poems and helped with editing.

Gratitude and dedication: Dale Wright

"Silences, edges" thanks to an email from Tom Kreilkamp
"Naming the Blank" for Ania Lifson
"Elegy, her voice" in memory of my mother
"Winter" by Van Gogh in memory of Joe Eck
"Silent Motives" for Barbara Herman
"On the phone she says" for Patricia Flumenbaum
"Arcata" for my sister, Nancy Ihara and in memory of Dan Ihara

Note to "Arcata, California": The marsh is part of an ingenious wastewater system; it was "terraformed" by bulldozers to be various depths, thus creating a "micro-terrain." Differing depths was necessary because if it was kept shallow, the tubers of the sago pondweed would spread everywhere uniformly and undermine the biodiversity needed for the marsh to do its work. Flow in the marsh is faster at the edges of groups of aquatic plants than in the middle. Vegetation was added to about one third of the last marsh, Hauser Marsh, to provide denser vegetation towards the end of the system. This ensures that the marsh will strip out any remaining solids in the effluent. Native Hardstem bulrush brought in from a nearby fishing lake. This marsh has alternating areas of open water and vegetation. Sago pondweed seeds were spread into all the deep areas of all the marshes. Ducks love to eat this seed, providing a natural harvest to keep it from taking over. The team learned a lot about planting, often by trial and error. Their greatest success came when they trucked in plants, cut off their tops, but kept a substrate of some of the original soil around them. Today it is a beautiful marsh full of various birds, otters, butterflies, and visitors.

Thank you to these magazines for publications:

"She heard Sparrows," "Pause," "The Shape of Silence," *Colorado Review* 43. 3.2016.

"Or just after" *New American Writing*, ed. Paul Hoover #33 2017.

"An alternate universe," *Boston Review* online March 29, 2017.

"Afterimage," "Et in Arcadia Ego," *Lana Turner*, January 10, 2017.

"Belonging to whom," "Property, "Increasing silence," "Metamorphosis, *Volt* 22, spring 2017.

"The Kiss," "Aftermath(Rothko)," "Breathless" *Web Conjunctions* August 8, 2017.

"Over Time" *Tupelo Quarterly* 14, 2017.

"The Shape of Silence," "The Startle of" *Dialogues*. 02: 52 Photographs & 25 Poems, ed. Aaron Stern, Jordan Sullivan & Will Schutt, New York, NY, Aaron Stern & Jordan Sullivan, 2018.

"Frantic" *Poem-a-Day*, June 26, 2018, ed. DA Powell.

"Agues and Fugues," *Paris Review*, May 2018.

"Paris de Nuit," "Interpretation," forthcoming, *Conjunctions.*

Martha Ronk is the author of 11 books of poetry and one book of short stories, *Glass Grapes*. Her most recent poetry books include *Transfer of Qualities*, Omnidawn 2013, long- listed for the National Book Award and *Vertigo*, Coffeehouse Press, 2007, winner of the National Poetry Series. She has had several artist residences at Djerassi and MacDowell, won a National Endowment Grant, and the Lynda Hull Poetry Award. Her PhD is in Renaissance literature and she has been a faculty member at Occidental College in Los Angeles and during the fall 2015 at Otis College of Art and Design.

Silences
by Martha Ronk

Cover art:
Untitled or Before the Curtain: Serenade by Courtney Gregg.
Ink, gesso, and graphite on paper (5" x 7 3/8"). 2018.

Cover typeface: Cochin LT Std
Interior typeface: Garamond 3 LT Std

Cover & interior design by Cassandra Smith

Printed in the United States
by Books International, Dulles, Virginia
On 55# Glatfelter B19 Antique
Acid Free Archival Quality Recycled Paper

Publication of this book was made possible in part by gifts from
Katherine & John Gravendyk in honor of Hillary Gravendyk,
Francesca Bell, and Mary Mackey,

Omnidawn Publishing
Oakland, California
Staff and Volunteers, Fall 2019

Rusty Morrison & Ken Keegan, senior editors & co-publishers
Kayla Ellenbecker, production editor
Gillian Olivia Blythe Hamel, senior poetry editor & book designer
Trisha Peck, senior poetry editor & book designer
Cassandra Smith, poetry editor & book designer
Sharon Zetter, poetry editor & book designer
Liza Flum, poetry editor
Matthew Bowie, poetry editor
Juliana Paslay, fiction editor
Gail Aronson, fiction editor
Rob Hendricks, *Omniverse* editor & marketing assistant
Clare Sabry, marketing assistant
Lucy Burns, marketing assistant
Hiba Mohammadi, marketing assistant
SD Sumner, copyeditor